Pirates on Lake Michigan?

by Lon Hieftje

ISBN-10: 1546493379

ISBN-13: 978-1546493372

Dedication

I dedicate this book to all us Michiganders that love Michigan history.

Those who have also wondered were there Pirates on the Great Lakes.

Author's note:

Many photographs are actual photos of a port, ship, and occasion. Some photos can't be found. I have tried to give you the best depiction that is possible.
Actual photographs are noted.

Yes, we did have pirates on the Great Lakes.

They generally stalked the Great Lakes in the mid-1800s to the early 1900s. It's true, on the Great Lakes, we had some of the most fearsome and burly pirates. These pirates ruled the fresh waters of the Great Lakes and made their living sailing and searching for treasures. Unlike the pirates that you see in the movies, our Great Lakes pirates were clean cut and normal looking. Their treasures were mostly lumber, illegal alcohol, and wild-game meat. Some pirates were known as Timber Pirates, moving illegal cut lumber from the Upper Peninsula to the eastern states.

It was a rough time on the Great Lakes where you didn't want to be confronted by one of these fearsome swashbucklers.

Our Pirates were clean-cut and looked like the common sailor of the time. When their ship would come up to you on the water or in your port, you wouldn't know if you were about to be taken. Their tactics were to sneak into ports, and sometimes all out forceful pirate style thievery taking over the ships in the ports, and on the Great Lakes.

We will start with John Rackham known as "Calico Jack Rackham" he was a small-time pirate from the 1700s. He became famous for stealing everything from fishing tackle right up to entire ships.

Frequent depiction of Calico Jack.

His style was to quietly slip in and take your ship in the darkness of night. You go out to your ship in the morning, and it's gone.

That was Calico Jack.

Calico Jack wanting to expand his territory looking for more lucrative plunder, he sailed out of the Great Lakes to warmer waters.

In October 1720, Calico Jack cruised near Jamaica, attacking numerous small fishing ships. He terrorized fishermen along the coastline. Calico Jack's ship was eventually attacked by an armed sloop and captured. Calico Jack and his crew were brought to Jamaica, where he and most of his crew were sentenced to be hanged.

In 1855, a religious gang was on and around Beaver Island on Lake Michigan. They burned down sawmills and stole $1,600 worth of goods from a local store on Beaver Island. This was done under the leadership of "King" James Jesse Strang. Strang took a self-proclaimed religious title of "President of the Church," Strang taught that the chief prophetic office embodied an overtly royal attribute, by which its occupant was to be not only the spiritual leader of his people but their King as well.

James Jesse Strang

He quickly made foes among his own people. One of them was Thomas Bedford, who was flogged for adultery on Strang's orders. It is also thought that just maybe he was flogged because Thomas felt considerable resentment toward the self-proclaimed "King."

keep them under the shadow of my wing & the cities from whence
my people have been driven shall be purged with a high hand for I will do it,
my people shall be again restored to their possessions but dark clouds are
gathering for the church is not yet wholly purged & now I command my
servants the apostles & priests & elders of the church of the saints that they
communicate & proclaim this my word to all the saints of God in all
the world that they may be gathered unto and round about the
city of Voree & be saved from their enemies for I will have a people to
serve me & I command my servant Moses Smith that he go unto the
saints with whom he is acquainted and unto many people & command
them in my name to go unto my city of Voree and gain inheritants
therein & he shall have an inheritants therein for he hath left all for
my sake & I will add to him many fold if he is faithful for he knows
the land and can testify to them that it is very good

— so spake the Almighty God of heaven

thy duty is made plain and if thou lackest wisdom ask of God in
whose hands I trust thee & he will give thee unsparingly for if
evil befall me thou shalt lead the flock to pleasant pastures

God sustain thee

Joseph Smith.

James J Strang

PS Write me soon & keep me advised of your
progress from time to time

Actual written letter.

Strang also had Dr. H.D. McCulloch excommunicated for drunkenness and other alleged misdeeds, after enjoying Strang's favors in Beaver Islands local government.

In June 1856, James Strang was waylaid around 7:00 PM on the dock at the harbor of the chief city of St. James, on Beaver Island, by a couple of Beaver Islands residents including Thomas Bedford, who shot him in the back. Not one person on board the ship made any effort to warn or aid James Strang.

In this book, I will take you through the life and activities of the most notorious Pirate of Lake Michigan. "Roaring" Dan Seavey.

The notorious Pirate of Lake Michigan.

Yes, an actually known Pirate did start his infamous adventures in Wisconsin, then on to Michigan's Upper Peninsula He was still alive after the Second World War. You probably have some questions, I will try to answer them as I take you through the Lake Michigan pirate's life - "Daniel Seavey."

Dan Seavey, also known as "Roaring" Dan Seavey, (March 23, 1865 – February 14, 1949) was a sailor, fisherman, farmer, saloonkeeper, prospector, U.S. marshal, thief, poacher, smuggler, hijacker, human trafficker, and notorious "Timber Pirate."

Actual photograph of Dan Seavey

This is Dan Seavey from his actual arresting mug shot. He does not look like most people's image of a Pirate. Actually, a good-looking fellow.

Daniel Seavey was a large and powerfully built man. He stood 6 foot 5 inches and weighed around 250 pounds. He was an intimidating man in size with huge hands, perfect for fighting. His hair was sandy in color, with a reddish complexion. He had a deep New England accent that would stand out when he spoke. Many towns on the shores of the Great Lakes have a story about Dan Seavey earning him the name, "Roaring Dan" that fit him well. He was known as a brawler and a bully, tall and vigorous and pugnacious. When confronted Dan would not back down, he would not stop until his opponent is down and out. He is the only Mariner to be branded as a Pirate on Lake Michigan. There were others with the lesser branding of Thieves and Scoundrels.

Captain Daniel Seavey spent the majority of his time on Lake Michigan docking in various ports.

South Haven, Michigan

Actual picture

Milwaukee, Wisconsin

Actual picture

Grand Haven, Michigan

Actual picture

Ludington, Michigan

Actual picture

Dan Seavey was born in Portland, Maine, on March 23, 1865. His father was a schooner captain. Dan quickly took to the sea himself at the age of 13, rather than junior high school.

Dan left home, at the age of 18 and became a sailor for the United States Navy for three years.

Actual picture

After his Navy duties, he became a deputy marshal for the Bureau of Indian Affairs.

He tracked bootleggers and smugglers on reservation lands in several states around the country.

Another story from that time as a marshal, Dan was pursuing a fugitive to the town of Naubinway in Upper Michigan, where Dan found the fugitive holed up in a local saloon. He told Dan that if a lawman could beat him in a fist fight, he would come quietly, so the two set to fisticuffs.

The fight reportedly went on for hours, with occasional breaks, to fortify themselves with whiskey. Eventually, Dan knocked the outlaw to the ground and then tipped the bar's piano on top of him. That ended the fight, but the fugitive's injuries were so severe that he died of them during the night.

It may have been this trip to Naubinway that inspired Dan to move to the Great Lakes. He moved near Marinette, Wisconsin in the late 1880s, where he married 14-year-old Mary Plumley and had two daughters. The family later moved to Milwaukee, Wisconsin, where Seavey fished, farmed and owned a local tavern.

An account from the Historical Society of Michigan describes that Frederic Papst of Papst Brewing Co. who Dan had been acquainted with, most likely through Dan's Tavern, encouraged him to head out to the Klondike Gold Rush.

In 1898, Dan Seavey pulled one of his disappearing acts without notice, he sold everything and left his family with nothing to participate in the Klondike Gold Rush.

He was unsuccessful and returned to the Great Lakes region around 1900. His Gold Rush adventurers went bust, and Seavey returned to Milwaukee in search of a new adventure.

He refused to pick up his family responsibilities and soon vanished onto Lake Michigan. Dan's wife later was thought to have remarried, changed her name to Mary Silver.

Dan's career as a Pirate begins.

Pirate Dan Seavey

In poverty, in the 1900s, Dan Seavey moved to Escanaba, Michigan and acquired a 42-foot two-mast schooner, which he named the Wanderer, and began his *career as a pirate.*

Dan's actual schooner "Wanderer."

In Escanaba, Dan married 22-year-old Zilda Bisner. This turned out to be a disastrous marriage when Bisner filed for divorce. She described how Seavey regularly beat her and made threats to her life. When Dan got wind of the divorce suit coming his way, Dan again disappeared into Lake Michigan on his schooner. A few years later Dan met and married Annie Bradley on the Garden Peninsula in Upper, Michigan, this marriage lasted many years.

Dan Seavey operated several businesses in Michigan, some legitimate and some not. Where ever he could see an easy dollar, he was all over it.

Through the years, he dabbled in lumber milling, logging, trapping, marine transporting, and prizefighting. On his pirate side, Dan also practiced smuggling, bootlegging, poaching, and other unmentionable activities. These activities made Dan Seavey a readily recognizable character in most ports, where today many stories can be recounted.

Roaring Dan was a well-known barroom brawler. At Manistee, Michigan, a resident thought he had beaten all local fighters and put out the word that he was seeking new challengers.

Picture not actually of Dan Seavey, but close to his stature, and the type of fighting.

Seavey quickly rose to the challenge and headed to Manistee, where he confronted his challenger in a local saloon. A battle then ensued, as Seavey flattened the Manistee man quickly and then hastily departed the scene before the authorities could arrive to assess the significant property damage. Dan Seavey occasionally fought for money.

His most famous prizefight occurred in Frankfort, Michigan, during the winter of 1904.

With considerable fanfare, Seavey battled Mitch Love, a respected professional boxer from downstate. The fight was held on the ice of the frozen harbor, where a shoveled circle served as a makeshift ring. About 200 people reportedly witnessed the contest, many placing sizable bets on the outcome.

The contestants went at it eagerly with bare knuckles for nearly two hours.

Seavey eventually made a bloody pulp of Love, who was carted off for medical attention by his dejected supporters. Roaring Dan apparently cleaned up on the contest, not only collecting the main purse but also a percentage of many side bets placed by his cohorts.

While living in Frankfort, he had an illegal fish trap offshore at the mouth of the harbor.

Other poachers would try to take from Dan's trap. Dan solved that problem by setting a line attached to the trap that rang a bell when touched.

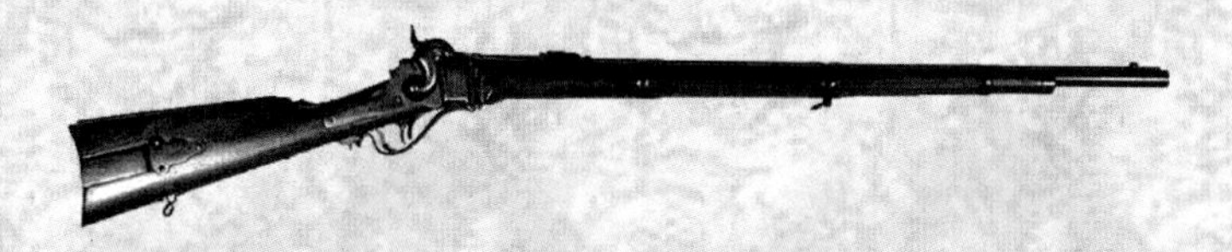

When the bell rang Roaring Dan, was a crack shot with a pistol, rifle, or shotgun, and would fire off a well-placed shot near the poacher. That ended any thievery of his poached catch.

This time Dan had no fixed home location, the entire Great Lakes became his home. He did whatever he could to make a profit using his schooner. He had a willing crew with complete disregard for both morality and social normal.

One of his dubious acts was to take advantage of the inability of local officials to enforce the law on the big lakes. He turned his schooner into a floating bordello. He would combine this by serving his customers smuggled liquor. It is rumored that not every girl working on his ship was there by choice.

Roaring Dan Seavey was notorious for altering sea lights, either by putting the lights out or placing false lights on a rocky shoreline.

This trick was known as "Moon Cussing" would cause ships to sail into rocks at night, where Dan's crew could swoop in and steal the cargo from the stranded vessel.

A significant amount of Dan's profit was made from venison poaching and theft.

Another group called Booth Fisheries attempted to compete with Roaring Dan's illegal venison trade. The story reported is that Dan managed to steal a cannon and mounted it on the Wanderer's deck. It is alleged that Roaring Dan attacked one of Booth's ships with the cannon, sinking it and killing everyone on board.

With this Dan made it clear that anyone else who tried to take over his operations would suffer the same fate.

Another story is about his raiding town's docks. He would take the Wanderer into a port in the dead of night, with no lights on and as little noise as possible.

His crewmen would quietly go onto the docks, grab everything not nailed down and head back to the ship before being noticed. Then quietly back onto Lake Michigan.

Dan's demise started in a bar in Grand Haven, Michigan. Grand Haven was a popular hub of the lumber trade, with logs coming down the Grand Trunk railroad to the docks where they were loaded on ships.

One ship was the Nellie Johnson, Dan found the Captain R.J. McCormic and his crew in the bar. With some socializing, Dan enticed the crew into

some serious drinking until they passed out. That was Dan Seavey's chance, Dan and his team headed to the docks to the loaded Nellie Johnson and sailed away.

Dan Seavey's reputation as a pirate was sealed on June 11, 1908, when he stole the schooner, Nellie Johnson.

They took the ship to Chicago trying to sell the wood on the black market, by the time Dan made it to Chicago, the word had been telegraphed of the theft, and nobody wanted to risk buying the lumber. So, Dan sailed north, being slowed down by the weight of the lumber.

On June 20, the federal cutter Tuscarora headed out of the Windy City in pursuit of Dan Seavey.

Actual photograph of the Cutter Tuscarora.

Captain Peterson Uberroth in command with McCormick, and U.S. Deputy Marshal Tom Currier with an arrest warrant with the charge of piracy. This warrant officially made Roaring Dan Seavey a Pirate in the history of the Great Lakes!

The Tuscarora was a 178-foot, steel hulled gunboat with the reputation of being the fastest ship on the Great Lakes. They cruised up Michigan shoreline, stopping in every port checking where ever Dan might be hiding. This proved to be slow with no luck in their searching.

Stopping in Ludington Captain Uberroth telegraphed all the lighthouses and lifesaving stations to the north, asking for their help in the search for Roaring Dan. Eventually, a station in Frankfort reported they had seen Dan in town. Late afternoon under cover of night the Tuscarora sailed north to Frankfort, fearing that one of Dan's many friends might warn him of their approach.

They arrived in Frankfort around dawn, where they anchored north of the

village below Point Betsie.

Roaring Dan had moored the Nellie Johnson and was again sailing in the Wanderer. That afternoon the schooner Wanderer was spotted sprinting out of the harbor under full sail.

The Tuscarora lifted anchor, gave chase at full speed, for hours. The Tuscarora ran at top speed so long the paint on the smokestack melted. The Tuscarora eventually caught up to the Wanderer when the wind slowed down, and Roaring Dan lost his speed. With a well-placed Cannon shot along the side of the schooner, Dan pulled to and surrendered seven miles southwest of Frankfort. They sent aboard an armed detachment of marines and brought Dan aboard the cutter Tuscarora and served Dan at the age of 43, with a warrant charging piracy, a crime which is punishable by death.

In irons, Roaring Dan Seavey was taken south to Chicago. On June 30, Dan Seavey was arraigned.

Instead of piracy, Roaring Dan Seavey was charged with mutiny and sedition of a vessel on which he had once been a seaman. Apparently, Dan had sailed on the Nellie Johnson years earlier. This saved the day and also having a lawyer who he had once taken on a hunting trip.

Despite under the government's best efforts, a grand jury failed to indict Roaring Dan Seavey on the charges, he was set free. One of Dan's defenses was that he won the ship fair and square in a poker game that night in Grand Haven, this is what Dan maintained for the rest of his life.

Although Dan's card was marked as a pirate, he wound up being enlisted to act, once again, as a U.S. deputy marshal on the Great Lakes for a short time. The government did this, on this theory that it takes a crook to catch a crook.

Was he true to his act as a U.S. marshal? You make that decision.

Roaring Dan continued to be an established character on the Great Lakes into the 1920s. In 1923 Dan was involved in a scheme to purchase some land at Gouley's Harbor on the Garden Peninsula, in the Upper Peninsula of Michigan. The plans were to establish a sportsman's club.

It never materialized. It was later found that the deed to the property being purchased was by John Silver and what was thought to be Dan's former wife Mary Silver. Who waved all dower rights to the property. The property being purchased by John Silver who was also known as Dan Seavey. As you recall that Dan's wife changed her name to Mary Silver after they parted ways. However, the deed shows that they never legally divorced. They may have rekindled their relationship under the disguise of John and Mary Silver. This choice of name may suggest that, in Dan's pirate life, Roaring Dan held his pirate life as a badge of honor. (Remember in the book "Treasure Island" John Silver.)

Dan later in Gouley's Harbor suffered a severe burn during a during a suspicious sawmill fire that claimed the lives of a couple men.

Due to his injury's, Dan retired from sailing in his 60s. Dan took up residency in Martha Champ Weed's boarding house near Escanaba, Michigan. Dan's lived quietly with his daughter Josephine in the later part of the 1930s into the 1940s.

The full story and truth of Dan Seavey's life and crimes may never fully come out. We do know that Dan was a master of the Great Lakes. Picture him in the nursing home as he would be looking out of his window at Lake Michigan. He probably would have been remembering his life as a Pirate along with the waves and the snapping of the sails of his schooner, the Wanderer.

Dan Seavey died in a nursing home in Peshtigo, Wisconsin in 1949 at the age of 84. Roaring Dan Seavey was buried next to his daughter, at Forest Home Cemetery in nearby Marinette, Wisconsin.

This is what Michigan was believed to be shaped back in the 1800s.

For my other books, please visit www.authorlon.com

Made in the USA
Middletown, DE
05 June 2021